PENGUIN WORKSHOP
An imprint of Penguin Random House LLC, New York

First published in the United States of America by Penguin Workshop,
an imprint of Penguin Random House LLC, New York, 2023

Copyright © 2023 by DGPH Studio

Visit us online at penguinrandomhouse.com.

Library of Congress Cataloging-in-Publication Data is available.

Manufactured in China

ISBN 9780593522318   10 9 8 7 6 5 4 3 2 1 TOPL

Design by DGPH Studio

Amazing
ANIMALS
Around the World

by DGPH Studio

Silky
anteater

Long-wattled
umbrellabird

Contents

Greater glider

Our Planet

It's estimated that 8.7 million different animal **species** (similar groups of organisms) live in the world, but only 2 million of them are currently known. From the grasslands to the hottest desert, from the arctic poles to the deepest rain forest, new species are discovered each year, helping us to understand their **environments** and how they have adapted to their surroundings. And different animal species also help teach us just how much our world has changed and evolved over time.

Creatures able to change their colors, grow armored defensive systems, and develop amazing hiding abilities and deadly poisonous hunting skills are amazing.

The animal kingdom is awesome!

Flying squirrel

Quetzal

Spoonbill

Greater superb bird-of-paradise

Banded linsang

Snake-necked turtle

Great hornbill

African paradise flycatcher

Giraffe

Long-eared bat

Lelwel hartebeest

Sumatran rhinoceros

Darwin's frog

Pallas's cat

Visayan warty pig

Fennec fox

Ecosystems

An ecosystem is the group of living species in a specific area that interact with one another and with their environment to form a community. The plant and animal species of an ecosystem depend on one another for their development. There are both land-based ecosystems and water-based ecosystems.

Land-based ecosystems, such as forests, grasslands, and deserts, can be classified by their plant and animal diversity. Depending on how dense the plant life is, ecosystems can vary greatly.

DESERT

An area of very scarce plant and animal species living in a dry climate.

TUNDRA

Made up of low-growth vegetation (**mosses**, **lichens**, grasses, and small shrubs), with a frozen **subsoil** and very low temperatures.

GRASSLAND

Open area covered in grasses that is usually in drier environments.

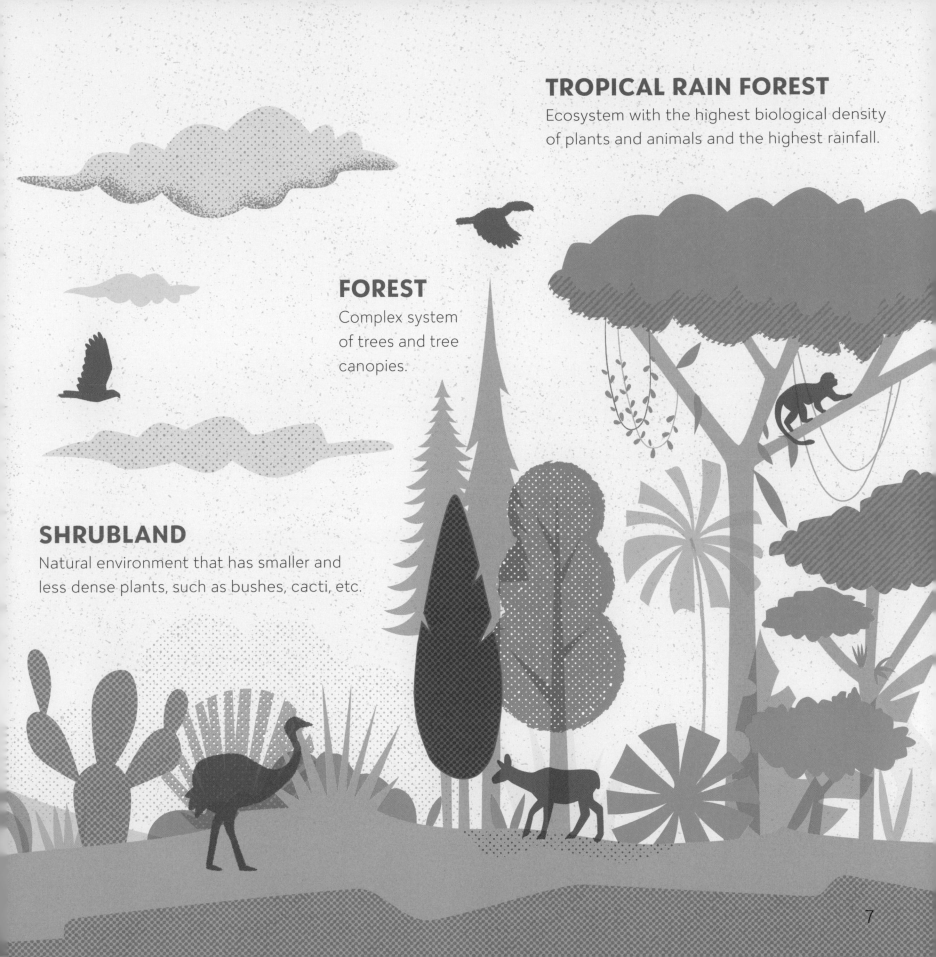

TROPICAL RAIN FOREST
Ecosystem with the highest biological density of plants and animals and the highest rainfall.

FOREST
Complex system of trees and tree canopies.

SHRUBLAND
Natural environment that has smaller and less dense plants, such as bushes, cacti, etc.

7

Around the World

The different species that live on earth represent its **biodiversity** (the variety of life found there).

Animals are everywhere! They adapt to many different climates and environments in creative and surprising ways. Although there is a greater diversity and quantity of animals in tropical climates, we can also find them in more extreme temperatures, such as the north and south poles, deserts, and high mountains.

Hellbender

Royal flycatcher

Glass frog

Saiga

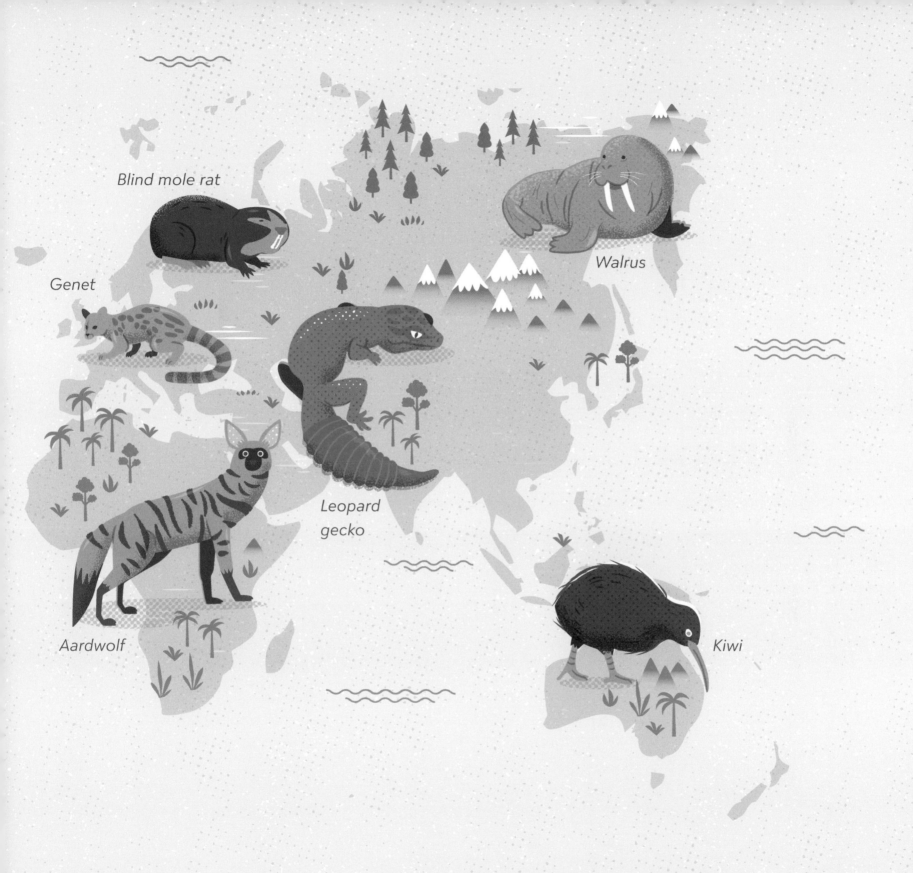

Blind mole rat

Walrus

Genet

Leopard
gecko

Aardwolf

Kiwi

9

Living in the Trees: Africa and Asia

There are many animals who are well adapted to spending practically their entire lives in the treetops, high above the ground. They eat, sleep, and nest in the tree branches. Some of them only go down to the ground to poop!

TARSIER

The tarsiers are one of the smallest leaping **primate** species in Southeast Asia, at only six inches long excluding their tails. Tarsiers have large goggling eyes, giving them amazing visual skills for their **nocturnal** activities, like hunting for insects, lizards, and snakes.

GOLDEN SNUB-NOSED MONKEY

The fur of the golden snub-nosed monkey allows it to live in the mountainous forests of central China at 9,000 feet of altitude and endure extreme temperatures. Their flat noses may have evolved to combat extreme cold. If they had an exposed nose, the cold would freeze them. The most striking thing about the golden snub-nosed monkey is the blue color of its face. It is one of the very few monkeys that have this color on their body.

WHITE-HANDED GIBBON

These incredible primates (the group of animals that includes humans) live in the tropical rain forest of Southeast Asia, and they have extremely long arms, which allow them to use a unique form of movement called **brachiation**. This means they move through the treetops swinging from branch to branch using only their arms.

When they walk, they do so on two feet, like humans, but they wave their arms over their heads for balance.

MADAME BERTHE'S MOUSE LEMUR

This species of tiny lemur is native to the island of Madagascar. It is the smallest of the primates, measuring only four inches long and weighing only one ounce! Due to its small size, it sometimes lives in abandoned bird nests.

PROBOSCIS MONKEY

Also known as the long-nosed monkey, the proboscis monkey is a tree-dwelling monkey with an unusually large nose that males use to attract their mates.

They can be found in the jungles of Borneo, close to rivers and swamps where they practice their amazing swimming abilities.

Living in the Trees: South America

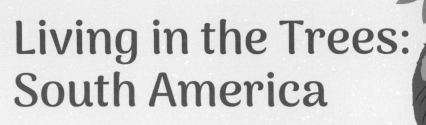

These monkeys can be found in the forest treetops of South and Central America, where they feed on leaves and fruits. They are known for calling and alerting other monkeys with a loud roaring sound.

Howler monkeys are one of the loudest animals in the world!

SAKI MONKEY

The white-faced saki monkey lives in the tropical rain forest regions in Brazil, Suriname, and Venezuela. And even though they are known as "white-faced" monkeys, only the male monkeys have white faces. The females do not.

If they feel threatened, they fluff up and shake their furry bodies!

BALD UAKARI

This monkey is characterized by the lack of hair on its face, forehead, and the upper part of its skull. The red color of their skin stands out in contrast to the rest of their body. They have very short tails and live in western Brazil and Peru.

THREE-TOED SLOTH

Similar in some characteristics to primates, but in actuality related to the anteater, the three-toed sloth spends most of the time high up in the branches of trees in tropical South American rain forests. They only travel down to the ground to poop. These **mammals** are one of the slowest animals in the world: They travel 120 feet per day, less than the length of a football field.

Up close, their fur has a green color due to the **algae** that sticks to it.

EMPEROR TAMARIN

The small Emperor Tamarin is one of the most adorable species of monkeys, averaging a body length of only nine inches long and weighing less than one pound. They can be found in the Amazon basin in moist tropical forests.

Why are they called emperor? It seems this species of tamarin's white moustache is very similar to that of Wilhelm II, the last emperor of Germany.

PYGMY MARMOSET

The adult pygmy marmoset weighs less than five ounces, making it the world's smallest monkey.

It has a long brown tail, similar to a squirrel's. And it even runs, quickly darts, and freezes like a squirrel. These fast little monkeys use their large tails to keep balance while galloping through the treetops.

AYE-AYE

Aye-ayes are only found on the island of Madagascar.

These animals are actually primates. They can grow about three feet long with tails longer than their bodies.

Aye-ayes spend their lives in the trees of the rain forest, avoiding going down to the ground. They are night creatures and during the day they rest in nests that they build with leaves and branches. They are characterized by having large eyes, thin fingers, and large sensitive ears.

WORST ENEMY

The main **predator** of the aye-aye is the fossa. The largest **carnivorous** animal native to Madagascar, they can reach nearly six feet in length including their tails. The fossa also feeds on lemurs and any other creature it can capture.

SHARP FINGER

One of the most prominent features of the aye-aye is its third finger, which is extremely thin. The third finger is used to pierce the outer skin of fruits and remove their pulp, as well as to extract insect larvae from branches and tree trunks.

15

They Fly, but They Are Not Birds

The animal kingdom is full of incredible creatures, and some have the ability to move through the air to travel great distances without feathers. They fly to reach the freshest leaves or to flee from a hungry predator.

FLYING FOX

The golden-crowned flying fox is the largest bat species; some reach a **wingspan** (the distance between the tips of their wings) of 60 inches. They can weigh up to two and a half pounds and travel more than 25 miles in a single night in search of food, mainly figs. They are so big that they fly with their pups clinging to their body.

SUNDA COLUGO

A skin membrane called the **patagium** that extends from their head, paws, and tails allows the Sunda colugo to glide from tree to tree in search of young leaves located in the tropical rain forest of Southeast Asia. It also allows them to cross distances of more than 200 feet.

SUGAR GLIDER

These small possums seem to have built-in parachutes! Sugar gliders in Australia and New Guinea can jump from tree to tree and glide the length of up to two tennis courts!

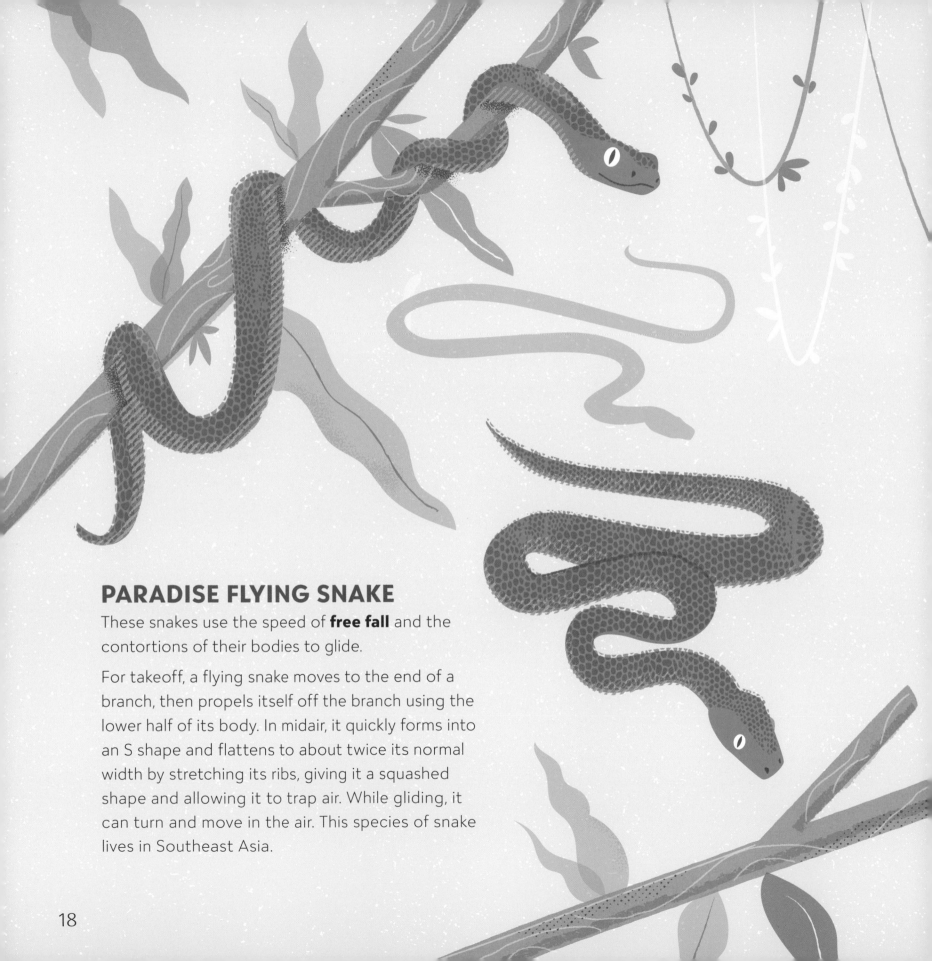

PARADISE FLYING SNAKE

These snakes use the speed of **free fall** and the contortions of their bodies to glide.

For takeoff, a flying snake moves to the end of a branch, then propels itself off the branch using the lower half of its body. In midair, it quickly forms into an S shape and flattens to about twice its normal width by stretching its ribs, giving it a squashed shape and allowing it to trap air. While gliding, it can turn and move in the air. This species of snake lives in Southeast Asia.

WALLACE'S FLYING FROG

Known as parachute frogs, these animals have huge webbed feet, allowing them to glide through the trees in Thailand, Malaysia, and Indonesia. When in danger or in search of **prey**, they jump off a branch and spread their four webbed feet to glide over to a neighboring tree, traveling 50 feet or more.

COMMON FLYING DRAGON

This small lizard can be found in tropical rain forests of Southeast Asia. Also known as the common flying dragon, it has extra skin that, when extended, functions just like the wings of a sugar glider to allow it to fly from one tree to another.

Armor and Scales

Protecting themselves against predators is a priority for any species. Spikes, large eyes, claws, **prehensile** (adapted to hold or grasp objects) tails, special hairs, and feathers are some of the features that animals develop to live within their environment. There are many animals covered with armor, powerful scales, spikes, or spines that they use to protect themselves from possible dangers.

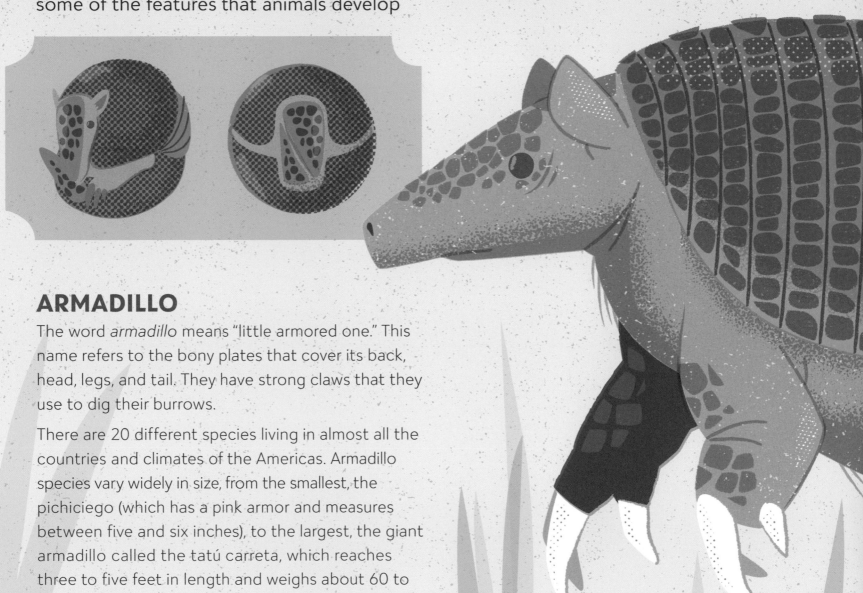

ARMADILLO

The word *armadillo* means "little armored one." This name refers to the bony plates that cover its back, head, legs, and tail. They have strong claws that they use to dig their burrows.

There are 20 different species living in almost all the countries and climates of the Americas. Armadillo species vary widely in size, from the smallest, the pichiciego (which has a pink armor and measures between five and six inches), to the largest, the giant armadillo called the tatú carreta, which reaches three to five feet in length and weighs about 60 to 100 pounds.

Tatú carreta

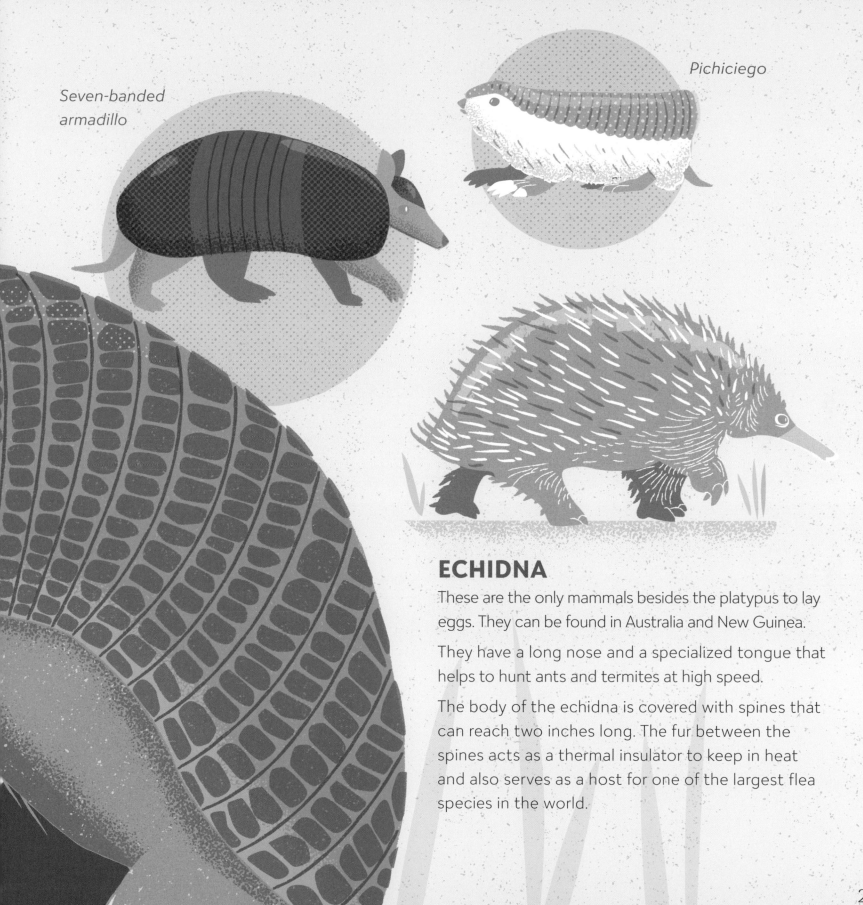

Seven-banded armadillo

Pichiciego

ECHIDNA

These are the only mammals besides the platypus to lay eggs. They can be found in Australia and New Guinea.

They have a long nose and a specialized tongue that helps to hunt ants and termites at high speed.

The body of the echidna is covered with spines that can reach two inches long. The fur between the spines acts as a thermal insulator to keep in heat and also serves as a host for one of the largest flea species in the world.

PANGOLIN

One of the most amazing creatures on earth is the pangolin. It can be found in tropical areas of Africa and Asia. It is the only scaled mammal on the planet.

Most of them live in the ground, but others, like the black-bellied species, climb trees. They are active at night.

Their complete scale coverage helps protect them against all predators in the wild except for humans.

Sadly, pangolins are one of the most illegally traded mammals in the world, making them an endangered species.

PANGOPUPS

When the newborns arrive, the mother carries them on her back, hanging onto her scales.

DEFENSE

Their name comes from the word *penggulung*, the Malay word for "roller," referring to this animal's defensive abilities. When it feels threatened, the pangolin will curl into a tight hard ball, protected by its sharp scales. Their scales are made of **keratin**, the same material as human fingernails!

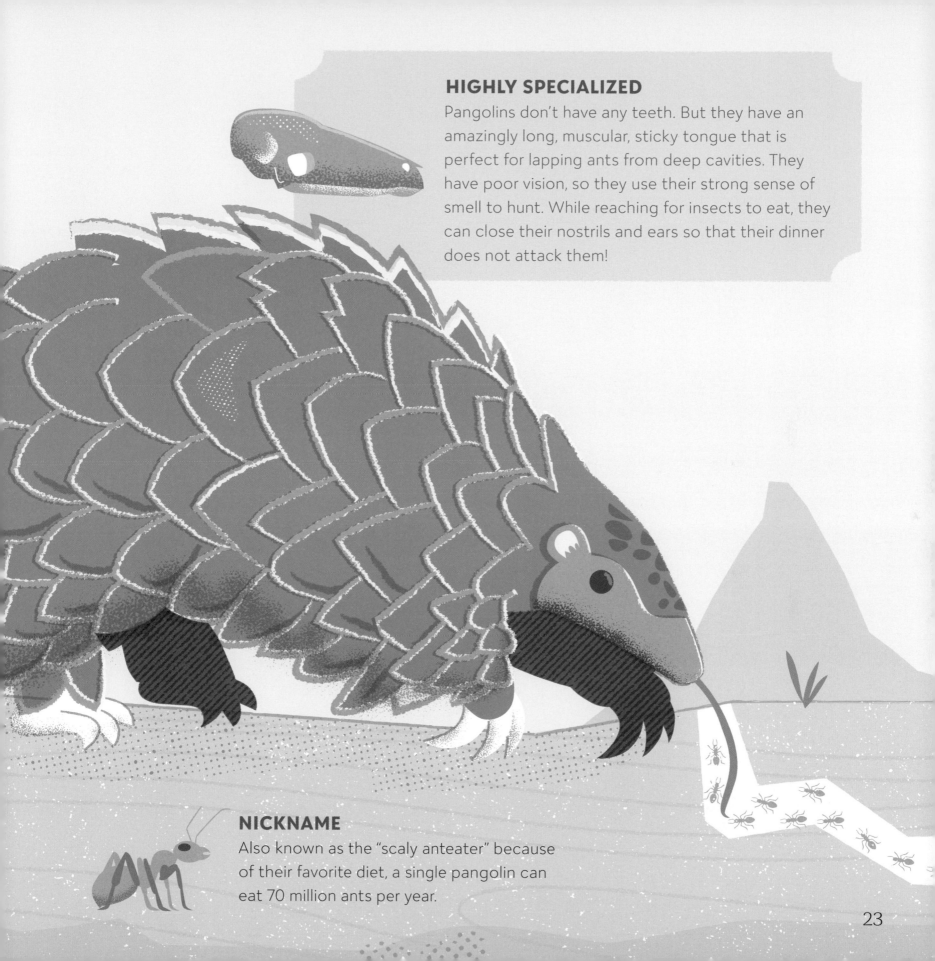

HIGHLY SPECIALIZED

Pangolins don't have any teeth. But they have an amazingly long, muscular, sticky tongue that is perfect for lapping ants from deep cavities. They have poor vision, so they use their strong sense of smell to hunt. While reaching for insects to eat, they can close their nostrils and ears so that their dinner does not attack them!

NICKNAME

Also known as the "scaly anteater" because of their favorite diet, a single pangolin can eat 70 million ants per year.

THORNY DEVIL

Behind that name and its strange appearance, there is a fascinating **reptile**, full of incredible abilities that allow it to live in one of the most extreme landscapes on earth: the Australian desert.

FREEZE!

This lizard can change color (from red to gray, orange, or yellow), stay frozen, or pretend to be a rock and blend in with its surroundings. They walk back and forth with slow jerky movements.

FALSE HEAD

A unique feature of the thorny devil, or thorny dragon, is the spiky "false head" on the back of their neck that serves to scare off predators.

SPONGE SKIN

When it rains or when there is any humidity in the environment, the thorny devil can absorb moisture from its skin and draw it to its mouth, allowing it to drink through its own skin. It is even able to walk into a puddle and transport water through the skin of its feet!

ARMADILLO GIRDLED LIZARD

These South African lizards have sharp and thorny scales on certain parts of their body. When a predator tries to attack, the armadillo girdled lizard curls its body into a circle, protecting itself from danger.

ALLIGATOR SNAPPING TURTLE

The shell of these turtles is really scary. It is very thick and ends in sharp-looking spikes.

Inside the mouth, this turtle has an extension on the tip of the tongue that imitates the shape of a worm, in order to attract fish.

This reptile is native to **freshwater** habitats in the United States.

25

Toxic and Deadly

We usually associate toxic venom with insect and snake bites. However, there are other animals that have sophisticated defense systems to help them escape from their predators, paralyze their prey, or even cause death.

SLOW LORIS

This is a very unusual animal with a venomous bite. The source of its venom is produced by a gland (an organ within the body) in the armpit. By licking that gland and mixing it with saliva, the loris activates the venom. They bite to ward off potential predators, and even apply venom to their babies' fur to protect them.

Slow lorises inhabit South and Southeast Asia and are cautious climbers. They move very slowly without producing any noise and without disturbing nearby vegetation. This is an especially effective way to get around without alerting predators.

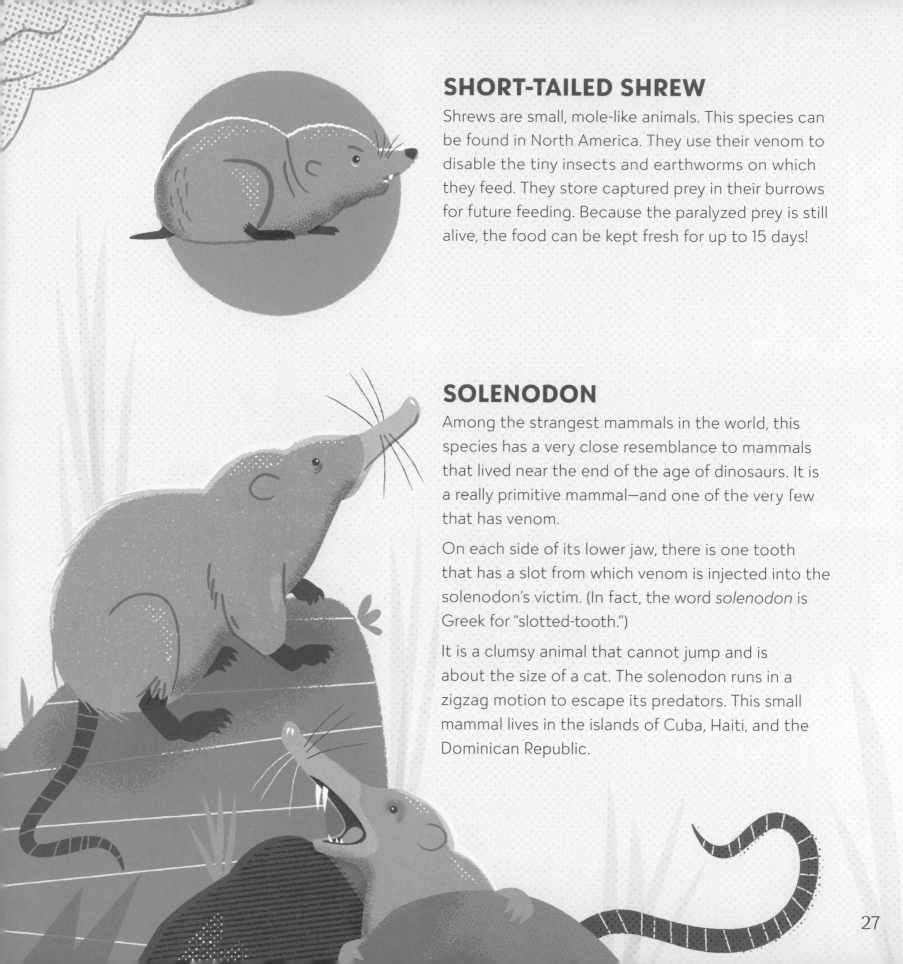

SHORT-TAILED SHREW

Shrews are small, mole-like animals. This species can be found in North America. They use their venom to disable the tiny insects and earthworms on which they feed. They store captured prey in their burrows for future feeding. Because the paralyzed prey is still alive, the food can be kept fresh for up to 15 days!

SOLENODON

Among the strangest mammals in the world, this species has a very close resemblance to mammals that lived near the end of the age of dinosaurs. It is a really primitive mammal—and one of the very few that has venom.

On each side of its lower jaw, there is one tooth that has a slot from which venom is injected into the solenodon's victim. (In fact, the word *solenodon* is Greek for "slotted-tooth.")

It is a clumsy animal that cannot jump and is about the size of a cat. The solenodon runs in a zigzag motion to escape its predators. This small mammal lives in the islands of Cuba, Haiti, and the Dominican Republic.

GILA MONSTER

The Gila monster's skin is black and rough, with bright, irregular pink, orange, or yellow marks. The short, thick tail stores fat that it uses to obtain energy during hibernation or when there is a shortage of food. These are venomous lizards found in the United States and Mexico.

Unlike snakes, which inject venom, these "monsters" latch onto their victims using their strong jaw and chew, allowing venom to flow into the open wound. The Gila monster moves with exaggerated slowness and is not very aggressive.

POISON DART FROG

The poison dart frog is considered to be one of the most poisonous animals on earth. At only about two inches long, it carries enough poison to kill 20,000 mice! It's bright coloration works to alert predators that it is toxic.

Some South American tribes apply the poison of this frog to the tips of their arrows and spears (hence its name *dart*), to be more effective—and deadly—when hunting.

HORNED LIZARD

Even though it has sharp spines and scales, this North American lizard can also squirt blood from its eyes to scare nearby predators!

KOMODO DRAGON

This is the largest lizard in the world, with an average length of nine feet and a weight of 155 pounds. It lives in Indonesia.

Komodo dragons hunt all kinds of prey, including reptiles, birds, and mammals up to the size of a water buffalo! But they also consume a lot of **carrion** (decaying dead animals), which, thanks to their powerful sense of smell, they can locate more than six miles away. These giant lizards have two venom glands in their jaws that secrete a toxin that causes muscle paralysis in their prey. In addition to that toxin, their saliva is an excellent breeding ground for all types of **bacteria**.

Living Fossils

Millions of years ago, dinosaurs inhabited the earth. After their extinction, life on the planet gave rise to new species. Only a few animals have remained mostly unchanged since then. Due to their appearance, they often remind us of dinosaurs.

CHINESE GIANT SALAMANDER

The appearance of this animal has not changed in the last 170 million years! This huge **amphibian** is the largest in the world, reaching the length of almost seven feet.

It has no **gills** or lungs, but is still able to breathe by sucking oxygen through its porous skin, keeping it always moist and sticky. The Chinese giant salamander lives in swampy places, between rocks along riverbanks, feeding on fish, worms, crabs, and even smaller salamanders, capturing them with impressive precision.

PURPLE FROG

Although it was recently discovered in 2003 in India, this frog (also known as the "pig-nosed frog" because of its peculiar snout) has maintained the same appearance for more than 120 million years.

The purple frog spends most of the year in burrows more than 10 feet deep that it builds using its shovel-shaped rear legs.

GHARIAL

These reptiles separated from all other crocodilian species more than 40 million years ago. They are found in the rivers of India and Nepal. Males have a lump on the end of their snouts, known as a ghara (Hindi for "mud pot"). They use their gharas to call out to each other and to blow bubbles during mating displays.

31

SHOEBILL STORK

Despite its prehistoric appearance, defiant attitude, and messy crest, the shoebill stork is not an aggressive animal. It belongs to the pelican family. This bird lives in Africa and is easily recognizable by its beak, which resembles a wooden shoe.

The shoebill stork can stand up to five feet tall and has a wingspan of over seven feet!

HOATZIN

Also known as the stinkbird, this Amazonian bird is clumsy when flying short distances and moving between the branches of the surrounding trees. Its digestive system is unique among other birds on the planet, using **fermentation** in the front part of its stomach to decompose the leaves and fruits it eats. For this reason, it gives off a strong—and foul—smell that serves as protection and makes it inedible to predators.

CASSOWARY

A spectacular and majestic animal that is known for the vivid colors on its head and neck and a dinosaur-like appearance, the cassowary has a large bony crest on top of its head, called a helmet, which can provide protection to the bird in dangerous situations. Due to its size, almost six feet in height, the cassowary cannot fly, but it has the ability to run at a very fast speed. This Australian bird is equipped with two huge claws (each with three toes, including one on each foot that functions like a four-inch dagger), making it one of the most dangerous in the world.

Long, Sticky Tongues

Having a very long tongue can be uncomfortable, but there are some animals that use their tongues as specialized tools to get food. These species have the ability to use the tongue as a hand, a weapon, or even a working tool.

AARDVARK

An aardvark's nose looks similar to a pig's. Its long tongue, amazingly adapted to smell food, can scoop up more than 50,000 ants and termites daily. An aardvark's tongue can grow up to 12 inches long.

They have very strong claws, specially adapted to dig holes, that help them find food and to build their burrows where they usually spend the day.

These African mammals are more closely related to elephants than to either pigs or anteaters!

ANTEATER

The anteater can be found in Central America and large regions of South America. It has a long, toothless snout and can ingest up to 35,000 ants and termites per day! It captures its meal thanks to an incredibly long and sticky tongue.

The anteater uses a set of sharp claws to tear open holes in the anthills and insert its 30-inch-long tongue rapidly in and out up to 160 times per minute! Ants fight back with painful stings, so the anteater can spend only a short time on each anthill. They never destroy an anthill, so that they can return to it in the future to feed again.

KINKAJOU

With its five-inch-long tongue, a kinkajou can easily extract honey from a hive or termites from their mounds. They are called honey bears but they also eat fruits and small mammals, which they catch with their nimble front legs equipped with sharp claws. They roam and eat at night, returning each morning to sleep in tree holes in rain forests of Central and South America.

WOODPECKER

All woodpeckers tend to have very long tongues, which help them capture insects to eat. The tongue is so long that it can't sit inside the bird's beak. Having its tongue wrapped around the back of its brain doesn't just give a woodpecker somewhere to store it; it also helps protect the bird's brain from injury during high-speed pecking.

NUMBAT

Numbats can be found in Southern Australia and are one of the most unusual **marsupials** (a specific group of over 250 mammals). They have incredibly long tongues and their diet is almost exclusively termites. They are able to eat up to 20,000 per day! Their specialized noses can detect underground galleries of termites. Their sticky tongues can reach into the soil to feed on insects living underground.

Wild Combinations

Elephant trunk, zebra legs, and rabbit ears? Beaver tail with saber teeth and pig body? Could these be real animals?

Some animals are so strange and amazing that they seem to be made up of different animal parts.

These combinations, although odd-looking, are the product of thousands of years of **evolution** allowing each animal species to survive, giving them superior skills to live in their environment and against their predators.

PLATYPUS

Considered to be one of the strangest animals in the world, the platypus has the unusual appearance of a duck's bill for a nose, a beaver's tail, and an otter's feet. This Australian swimming mammal confused European naturalists when they first saw it.

EGGS AND MILK

Platypus are able to both lay eggs and feed their cubs milk. These are two qualities that apparently do not exist in any other animal.

BIOFLUORESCENCE

The platypus's fur glows green under ultraviolet light. They are believed to have developed biofluorescence (the ability to absorb and radiate light) to adapt to lowlight conditions and therefore be able to interact with each other in the dark.

VENOMOUS STING

Males have venomous spurs that can cause immediate pain.

RUBBERY BEAK

Their beak is completely different than those of birds. In fact, the platypus beak is a unique organ that allows it to detect prey underwater, including shrimps, worms, crustaceans, and mollusks.

OKAPI

This calm and shy animal lives in the Congolian rain forest. It has a body similar to a horse's, the head and horns of a giraffe, and zebra-stye black stripes on its legs and tail. Okapis can use their long tongues to clean their ears.

GERENUK

The name means "giraffe-necked" in the Somali language of the eastern African region where this species of gazelle lives. They have large eyes and long ears like rabbits.

Gerenuk feed standing on their hind legs and extending their long necks. They are able to stay in this position for a long time and even walk a certain distance standing upright!

TUFTED DEER

The most amazing feature of this deer, which lives in central China, is the pair of fangs (just under an inch long!) that protrude from its mouth on each side. Although these teeth may resemble the fangs of a saber-toothed cat, the truth is that tufted deer are very peaceful animals.

TAPIR

Tapirs are large mammals with pig-like bodies, legs like a rhinoceros's, and short trunks that resemble those of elephants. In reality, this species is most closely related to horses.

PANDA STYLE

The Malayan tapir is characterized by having black-and-white skin, similar to that of a panda. The other four species of tapir live in Central and South America and have dark brown skin.

FARMING STOMACH

They are excellent seed dispersers for some plant species. After they pass through the digestive tract, and the tapir moves throughout the rain forest, seeds are left along with the animal's droppings on the ground to grow new plants.

UNIQUE NOSE

Their large snouts help tapirs to pluck leaves, grasses, roots, and **aquatic** plants—their main sources of food.

BABY CAMO

At birth, tapir babies have dark fur dotted with white spots and lines. This helps them to be **camouflaged** (hidden) in the dappled sunlight of the rain forest. As the young tapirs grow, they begin to acquire the typical coloration of adults.

MANED WOLF

This South American mammal, although it looks like a mix of fox and wolf, is not actually related to either species. Their closest living relatives are bush dogs.

STILTS

One of the most striking characteristics of this animal is its very long legs, similar to a deer's. This adaptation allows them to see over tall grasses when hunting. Its long legs also allow the maned wolf to run fast and jump high.

ALMOST VEGGIE

Even though it belongs to the dog family, the maned wolf prefers to consume small prey such as **rodents**, reptiles, insects, and medium-size birds. But it also consumes large amounts of fruits—up to 50 percent of its diet.

HORSE RIDE

The gait of the maned wolf is similar to that of a trotting horse. It moves forward by using the limbs on the same side at the same time: right front and back legs move together, then left front and back legs. This allows the wolf to travel long distances while saving energy.

Now You See Me, Now You Don't

Nature is full of living beings that blend in with their environments in very creative ways. Camouflage is an adaptation that helps animals disappear into the scenery in which they live. Being almost invisible, they can avoid being caught by their predators, increasing their chances of survival.

But predators can also use camouflage. When predators track their prey, if they are well camouflaged, they are better prepared to make a surprise attack.

POTOO

Also known as a ghost bird, due to the difficulty in finding it, the potoo is a very mysterious bird!

FUNNY FACE

The potoo has a set of large, disturbing yellow eyes, which help it to hunt insects at night. Although the potoo's mouth is very large and wide, its beak is quite small and disproportionate for the size of its head.

CAMOUFLAGE MASTER

The feather colors of the potoo are grayish and brown with black and white spots, and look very much like the texture of tree bark. During the day it perches upright without moving on a tree log, resembling part of the stump.

GHOST HOWL

When night falls in the depths of Central and South American rain forests, the potoo looks for food and sings a sad melody (*auuuh auuuuuuh!*), similar to a human moan. This song is a part of many Latin American folk legends.

HUMPTY DUMPTY

The potoo only lays a single egg that is white with purplish spots. This is one bird that doesn't build any type of nest. It uses great care to place its lone egg on the upper part of a log or a broken branch.

LEAF-TAILED GECKO

These nocturnal rain forest creatures live on the island of Madagascar and have long flat bodies that can be up to three inches long. They have triangle-shaped heads with large golden eyes and broad, flat leaf-like tails. These reptiles feed on insects and invertebrates like land snails.

Their skin has a mottled pattern with a variety of colors like greens, browns, oranges, and even purples depending on the habitat.

They are experts at avoiding predators because their skin can look exactly like a tree branch. They are able to flatten their bodies against a tree so that they do not even cast a shadow. In this way, the leaf-tailed gecko can disappear almost completely.

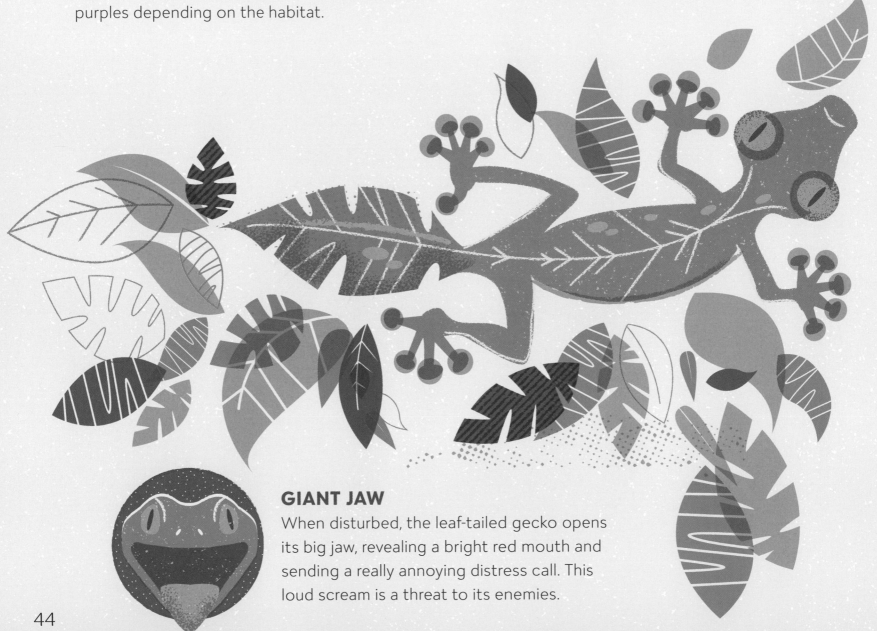

GIANT JAW
When disturbed, the leaf-tailed gecko opens its big jaw, revealing a bright red mouth and sending a really annoying distress call. This loud scream is a threat to its enemies.

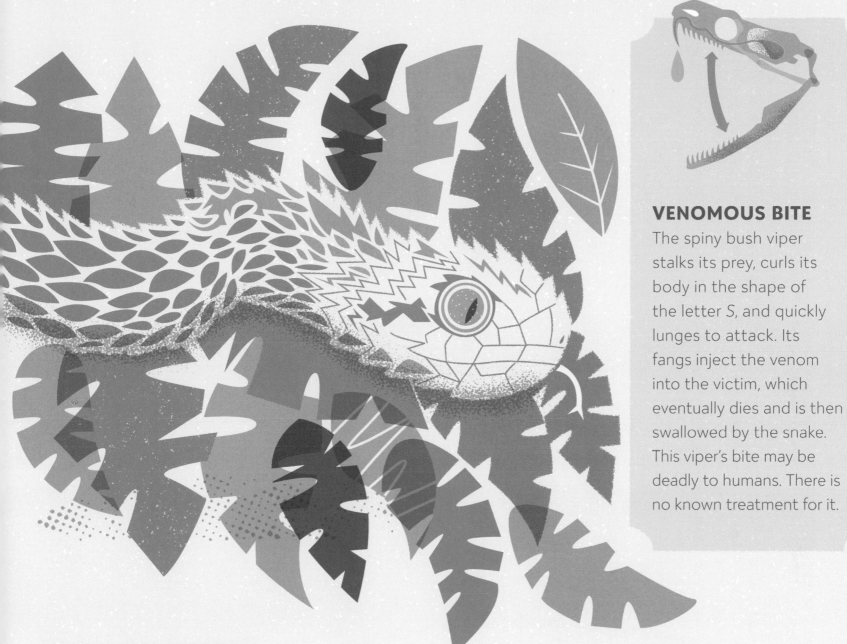

VENOMOUS BITE

The spiny bush viper stalks its prey, curls its body in the shape of the letter S, and quickly lunges to attack. Its fangs inject the venom into the victim, which eventually dies and is then swallowed by the snake. This viper's bite may be deadly to humans. There is no known treatment for it.

SPINY BUSH VIPER

The spiny bush viper is covered with sharp scales, giving it a uniquely "spiky" look. These relatively small snakes (only growing up to 30 inches) move silently while climbing trees, using their tail to hold onto branches or hang upside down.

These reptiles are nocturnal creatures, spending most of the daytime on trees or hiding in foliage, where they wait to ambush their victims, including birds, rodents, frogs, lizards, and even other snakes.

These amazing venomous vipers are rarely seen and can only be found in central Africa.

CHAMELEON

If there is one true expert in camouflage, it is the chameleon. This species of lizard has the ability to change color so that it can blend in with its surroundings, reveal its mood, and communicate with other chameleons. They live in warm habitats in Africa, southern Europe, and Southeast Asia.

360-DEGREE VISION

Chameleons can move their cone-shaped eyes independently of each other, allowing them to have a 360-degree field of vision. This means they can see in all directions at once.

LEGS AND TAIL

The feet of chameleons are highly adapted to living in trees and bushes. Their tails and fingers help them stay balanced.

FASTEST TONGUE

The chameleon has the potential to extend its sticky tongue up to twice the length of its body, unrolling it at an amazing speed. It takes about 20 milliseconds to catch a cricket!

JACKSON'S CHAMELEON

Three horns, located on the nose and above each eye, make these chameleons look like small *Triceratops* dinosaurs.

BROOKESIA NANA

The smallest chameleon species grows only to a length of half an inch.

LANCED-NOSED CHAMELEON

Also known as Pinocchio for its long, pointed, and flexible nose, this reptile has distinctive purple, blue, and green colorful spots.

CAMPAN'S CHAMELEON

The jeweled chameleon is named for its amazing ornate design.

VEILED CHAMELEON

This chameleon lives in hot and dry areas and has a special hump on its head that allows it to collect water.

Giant vs. Tiny

From a tiny frog to a bird that is almost ten feet tall, the diversity of animal sizes is huge! This is due to the ways in which they have adapted to changes in their environments over time.

New species are still being discovered today, and occasionally new records are established for the largest and smallest species.

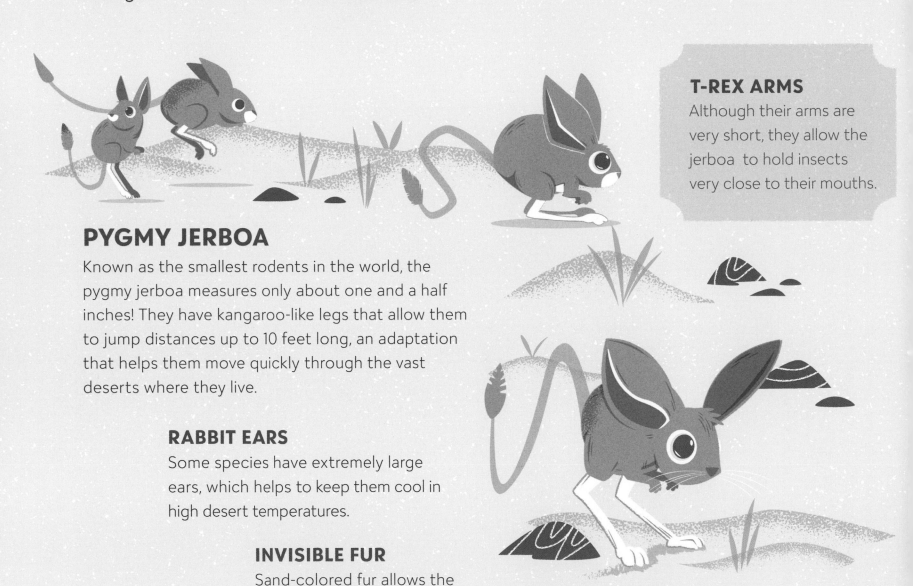

T-REX ARMS
Although their arms are very short, they allow the jerboa to hold insects very close to their mouths.

PYGMY JERBOA

Known as the smallest rodents in the world, the pygmy jerboa measures only about one and a half inches! They have kangaroo-like legs that allow them to jump distances up to 10 feet long, an adaptation that helps them move quickly through the vast deserts where they live.

RABBIT EARS
Some species have extremely large ears, which helps to keep them cool in high desert temperatures.

INVISIBLE FUR
Sand-colored fur allows the pygmy jerboa to blend with its surroundings.

JUMPING AWAY
They can jump in zigzag patterns to confuse predators.

CAPYBARA

The largest living rodents in the world weigh up to 165 pounds and measure almost four and a half feet long. Capybaras are semiaquatic (living both on land and in water) mammals that are found in almost all the countries of South America.

FERRY RIDE

Since they are excellent swimmers, other smaller animals use them as transportation and hop on their backs to cross rivers and ponds.

SUBMARINE SKILLS

Capybaras' eyes, ears, and nose are positioned on the top of the head, which means they have excellent sight, hearing, and smell even while swimming. When in danger, capybara can sink below the water's surface, leaving only those important parts of the body exposed to hide from predators. They can also dive and stay underwater for up to five minutes.

DISGUSTING DIET

The capybara's diet is mainly aquatic plants and grass. But they can also eat their own poop! This provides them with helpful bacteria that process the thick fibers in their meals.

GOLIATH FROG

This amphibian gets its name due to its size, being the largest frog in the world. These incredible creatures can grow as large as a domestic cat. They can jump up to ten feet. Even though they grow quite large, their eggs and tadpoles are the same size as other frogs.

This frog is normally found in and near rivers in Cameroon and Equatorial Guinea.

Eggs

Tadpole

Tadpole with two legs

Froglet

Adult frog

50

PAEDOPHRYNE AMAUENSIS

This tiniest of frogs is only about a third of an inch long and can sit on top of a dime!

Discovered in 2009, the *P. amanuensis* can jump 30 times their own body length.

Extremely difficult to find, they camouflage themselves among dead leaves in the rain forests of Papua New Guinea.

BEE HUMMINGBIRD

This small hummingbird, less than two inches long, is often mistaken for a bee. It is also known as a fly bird or bee elf.

It has the second-fastest heart rate of all animals and is also the bird with the fewest feathers. The bee hummingbird lives on the island of Cuba, and has the highest body temperature of all birds, exceeding 104 degrees Fahrenheit.

MICRO

Due to the smallness of these birds, their nests are never larger than a walnut shell. Their eggs are only the size of a pea!

STEADY FLIGHT

In flight, the bee hummingbird can flap its wings about 80 times per second, which allows it to stay in the air in the same position for a long time. This allows it to suck the **nectar** from flowers without needing to lean or sit on them.

NEEDLE BEAK

The beak of the bee hummingbird is black and very thin. Their diet is mainly nectar and insects. And their extremely long tongues help them search deep inside flowers to find them.

OSTRICH

The ostrich is the largest and heaviest bird in the world. It can reach a height of nearly 10 feet tall and more than 300 pounds. It can be found in semidesert areas of Africa.

CHICKEN WINGS

Due to their small wings, ostriches cannot fly. Even so, their wings help them to propel their bodies forward, to balance when running, and to scare possible predators away.

AMAZING DANCER

When he wishes to mate, the male ostrich performs an elaborate mating dance to impress the female bird. He bows and crouches down, stretches his wings, and displays his feathers, shaking wings and tail. If the female is interested, the two ostriches will mate.

FAST AS LIGHTNING

With speeds of up to 44 miles, the ostrich is the fastest two-legged animal in the world. Their legs can help them to travel up to sixteen feet in a single stride!

MYTH

Sometimes an ostrich will lower its head to the ground to go unnoticed in the presence of predators. But it is simply not true that the ostrich buries its head when it feels it is in danger.

MACRO

An ostrich egg weighs between 2.2 and 4.5 pounds (equivalent to about two dozen chicken eggs). These eggs are the largest of all bird eggs, each measuring six inches long.

53

Conservation

Currently about 40 percent of the animal species that inhabit the planet are at risk of disappearing forever. This is due to the action of humans on nature and its biodiversity. Conserving our planet is essential for our survival and that of all living beings that live on it.

CONGO JUNGLE

The second-largest jungle on the planet, the Congo Basin, contains a quarter of the tropical rain forests that still remain in the world. Due to its size, it is possible to find dry forests, prairies, savannas, and high mountain forests within this region. It has huge areas that have not been explored by humans.

FOREST OF BORNEO

The island of Borneo contains a huge humid forest with some of the most recently discovered species of amphibians, plants, and trees.

AMAZON RAIN FOREST

The most vital of our "green lungs," the Amazon is the largest tropical rain forest in the world. It houses many plant and animal species that have not been discovered yet.

GREEN LUNGS

Green lungs can be small areas of parkland in urban areas or huge regions of forest or rain forest. They act as filters and also add new oxygen into the air. They are vital to the health and survival of all living things.

And they act like a sponge that absorbs **carbon dioxide** (the polluting gases produced mainly by industrial and automotive activity).

AFRICAN SAVANNA

A huge area in central Africa covered with grasslands and shrubs, this open field is home to many of the largest land animals in the world.

GREAT BARRIER REEF

Made up of more than 600 types of **corals**, the world's largest reef can be seen from outer space. It has a vast biodiversity that is being affected by global warming.

RUSSIAN TAIGA

This forest does not have a great plant or animal diversity, but its large area of **conifers** such as pine trees makes it one of the main green lungs of the planet.

OCEANS

Oceans are one of the main biodiversity reserves in the world. They make up 99 percent of the habitable space on the planet and contain nearly 250,000 known species and many more that are yet to be discovered.

The oceans and the life they contain are essential to the health of our planet, supplying half the oxygen we breathe and absorbing large amounts of human-made emissions of carbon dioxide in the atmosphere each year.

ARCTIC AND ANTARCTICA

The north and south poles are the refrigerator of the world, balancing the temperature of our planet. In addition, the ice found there is the largest reserve of fresh water on this planet.

Glossary

Algae: Non-flowering and typically aquatic plants, including seaweed. Algae are indispensable because they produce about half the oxygen in Earth's atmosphere.

Amphibian: Cold-blooded vertebrate animals that spend the first part of their life in water breathing through gills, and their adulthood on land breathing through lungs. They are distinguished by undergoing a transformation during their development (known as metamorphosis).

Aquatic: Living in or near water. It refers to animals, such as fish, crabs, or whales, and to ecosystems such as lagoons, seas, or wetlands.

Bacteria: Microscopic organisms that are not visible to our eyes. Bacteria are the most abundant organisms on the planet. They can live in a variety of environments, from hot water to ice. Some bacteria are good for you, while others can make you sick.

Biodiversity: A term used to describe the enormous variety of life on earth. It refers to every living thing, including plants, bacteria, animals, and humans. It can also be used to refer to all of the species in one region or ecosystem.

Biofluorescence: The ability of some organisms to absorb energy from light and then remit it at a longer wavelength, resulting in a soft glow with colors including blues, greens, and reds.

Brachiation: A form of movement in which primates swing from tree to tree using their arms. This kind of skill is only achieved by gibbons of Southeast Asia, and is also known as arm swinging.

Camouflage: An adaptation—usually of color or patterns—that helps certain animals "disappear" into the environment in which they live.

Carbon dioxide: A colorless and odorless gas produced by burning carbon and organic elements. It is naturally present in air and is absorbed by plants in photosynthesis. The burning of fossil fuels and deforestation have caused a serious increase in the atmospheric concentration of carbon dioxide, raising the atmospheric temperatura and triggering global warming.

Carnivore (carnivorous): An animal that mostly eats other animals.

Carrion: The decaying flesh of dead animals. It is an important food source for large carnivores and omnivores.

Conifer: A type of evergreen tree or shrub that never loses its leaves. They produce oval-shaped fruit called cones. Conifers have needle-shaped or scale-like leaves.

Coral: Small invertebrate animals that often live at the bottom of tropical seas. Millions of individuals connected together form colonies called reefs.

Environment: Everything that surrounds us forms the environment. All animals, plants, weather conditions, soil, rocks, and water are parts of the environment.

Evolution: The process by which life originated on earth, and which has given rise to the enormous diversity of living beings that we find on our planet. Evolution is the gradual change of living beings and other objects in the natural world. It primarily affects animals and plants, but also rocks, planets, stars, and everything that exists in nature.

Fermentation: A process (that does not require oxygen) in which a substance breaks down into a simpler substance. Microorganisms like yeast and bacteria usually play a role in the fermentation process, creating foods like beer, wine, bread, kimchi, and yogurt.

Free fall: Any object moving freely under only the influence of gravity.

Freshwater: Any water that is not salty. This includes water found in lakes, streams, rivers but not the ocean. It is also a term used for water that is suitable for human consumption.

Gills: The main organs of respiration for animals that live in or under the water and are equivalent to lungs.

Herbivore (herbivorous): An animal that only eats plants and their juices. They also feed on fruits, roots, or seeds.

Keratin: A hard protein that gives structure to certain body parts in humans and animals. Our nails and hair are made up of keratin, as are claws, horns, feathers, beaks, and shells.

Lichen: Various small plants composed of a particular fungus and a particular algae growing together, typically forming colored patches on sponges, rock, wood, and soil.

Mammal: Vertebrate animals (including humans) that breathe through their lungs. Females feed their young by secreting milk, which helps the animals grow strong and healthy.

Marsupial: A large group of mammals in which the females have a pouch or marsupial bag, which serves to protect the babies while they complete their growth.

Moss: A class of plants that lack true roots. They grow in humid environments, forming a layer on the earth, rocks, tree trunks, and in water.

Nectar: A sweet liquid substance that flowers produce to attract insects and animals that carry out pollination (transport of pollen from one flower to another). Nectar is the food of different animal species and the most important raw material for the production of honey for the honeybee.

Nocturnal: Animals that are awake and active at night and that rest during the day. They hunt, feed, or mate at night and sleep and hide during the day.

Omnivore (omnivorous): An animal that eats both plants and other animals.

Patagium: A membrane or fold of skin between the forelimbs and hind limbs on each side of bats or gliding mammals and lizards.

Predator: An animal that hunts, catches, and eats other live animals to eat. The top predator is the one that is not prey for other animals.

Prehensile: A limb that has adapted for seizing, grasping, or holding, especially by wrapping around an object.

Prey: Animals that are hunted for food. The prey is what the predator eats.

Primate: A group of mammals to which humans and their closest relatives belong. They share similar characteristics: five fingers and toes, mobility of the fingers, especially the thumb, and flat nails (they do not have claws).

Reptile: Animals that are characterized by having skin with scales or by a protective shell. They are all oviparous, meaning that they hatch from an egg.

Rodent: The biggest group of mammals, with approximately 2,280 current species. Most rodents are short-legged, quadruped, and are relatively small. Their main common characteristic is the two incisor teeth, which are large and continuously growing. Rodents are mostly herbivores.

Species: A specific kind of organism. Species is a basic classification for living things that all share common characteristics. All animals or plants that are the same kind are one species: Dogs are one species. Wolves are another species. Humans are another species.

Subsoil: A layer of soil that is just below the surface of the ground, but above the hard rock layer. It is composed of substances such as clay and sand.

Wingspan: The distance between the tips of the wings of a bird, insect, bat, or aircraft at their widest point.